Stomp!

For Jocelyn – J.W.
For Steph and Summer – P.H

ORCHARD BOOKS
338 Euston Road, London NW1 3BH
Orchard Books Australia
Level 17/207 Kent Street, Sydney, NSW 2000

First published in 2011 by Orchard Books
First published in paperback in 2012

ISBN 978 1 84616 795 9

A CIP catalogue record for this book is available from the British Library.

2 4 6 8 10 9 7 5 3 1

Printed in China

Orchard Books is a division of Hachette Children's Books,
an Hachette UK company.

www.hachette.co.uk

Stomp!

Jeanne Willis
Paul Howard

ORCHARD

Knock!
Knock!

Who's there?

A
mini
monster!

Stomp! Stomp!

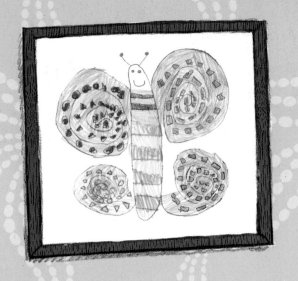

Here he comes, down the hall.

3

smashing
plates!

He's looking
for something,
but it's not there.

Stomp! Stomp!

Off he goes
to the playroom.

Blowing trumpets!

Booting footballs!

Tooting hooters!

He's looking
for something,
but it's not there.

Stomp!
Stomp!

Up he goes
to the bathroom.

Flinging flannels!

He's looking
for something,
but it's not there.

Stomp!
Stomp!

Off he goes

to Baby's room.

Monster **stops**.

Monster **stares** . . . .

"It's there! It's there!"

"That's MY teddy!"

roars Monster.

"Oooh! Mine!"

says Baby.

Stomp!

Off he goes . . .

Stomp!

. . . home with Teddy.